46 Consumer Reporting Agencies Investigating You

Table of Contents

Disclaimer

This booklet is intended to provide general information and should not be considered legal, tax or financial advice. It's always a good idea to consult a legal, tax or financial advisor for specific information on how certain laws apply to you and about your individual financial situation.

Introduction

You should know that a consumer reporting agency" or CRA means any person which, for monetary fees, dues, or on a cooperative nonprofit basis, regularly engages in whole or in part in the practice of assembling or evaluating consumer credit information or other information on consumers for the purpose of furnishing consumer reports to third parties and which uses any means or facility of interstate commerce for the purpose of preparing or furnishing consumer reports. (15 USCS § 1681a).

You should know there are more than the three major consumer reporting companies (Equifax, Experian and TransUnion). There are also many specialty consumer reporting agencies. All of these consumer reporting companies you are about to discover collect information, compile it and subsequently provide (sell) these reports to other companies telling them all about you.

A creditor, as defined by the Fair Credit Reporting Act (FCRA) as a company that furnishes information to consumer reporting agencies. Typically, these are creditors, with which a consumer has some sort of credit agreement (such as credit card companies, auto finance companies and mortgage banking institutions).

If the report being compiled is an "investigative consumer report" this means it includes information on a consumer's character, general reputation, personal characteristics, or mode of living as obtained through personal interviews with neighbors, friends, or associates of the consumer reported on or with others.

If the report is an Employment background check also known as a consumer report; they can include information from a variety of sources, including credit reports, driving record, criminal records checks, criminal background checks. Additionally, public records – such as bankruptcy filings and other court documents and information related to your employment history.

The companies using data compiled/added into your consumer reports make what they feel are informed decisions about you. The data in these files are highly relative to your ability to get credit, employment, residential rental housing, insurance and in perhaps, many other decision-making situations that arise concerning you. Because of this cycle, you need to be very concerned about the accuracy of these multitude of consumer reports.

The list compiled below includes the three nationwide consumer reporting companies and many other consumer reporting companies that focus on certain market areas and consumer segments. The list gives you tips about how you can determine which of these companies may be important to you. It also makes it easier for you to take advantage of your legal rights to

(1) obtain the information in your consumer reports, and

(2) dispute suspected report inaccuracies with companies as needed.

This list is current as of January 2018. It includes entities that have identified themselves as consumer reporting companies or have indicated when they provide consumers access to their personal consumer reports. The list incorporates information from the companies' own self-descriptions that has not been independently verified by the Bureau. This list does not cover every company in the industry. It is not intended to be all-inclusive.

Nor does this list reflect determinations as to whether any particular entity is subject to the Fair Credit Reporting Act. Furthermore, presence on, or absence from, this list does not indicate whether the consumer reporting company is subject to the Bureau's supervisory or enforcement authority. To provide your suggested corrections or additions to the list, contact the Bureau at info@consumerfinance.gov and include "Attn: Jonah Kaplan" in the subject line.

Who can see your consumer reports?

Consumer reporting companies must follow legal restrictions but generally can provide consumer reports and risk scores to an array of businesses, including:

☐ Lenders (including those that offer credit cards, home, payday, auto (including auto leasing) and student loans)

☐ Employers, volunteer organizations, and government agencies to determine eligibility for government assistance (employment and background screening)

☐ Landlords and residential real estate management companies (tenant screening)

☐ Banks, credit unions, payment processors and retail stores that accept personal checks (check screening)

☐ Companies that market and sell products and services specifically to lower-income consumers and subprime credit applicants, such as short-term lending and rent-to-own businesses among others

☐ Debt buyers and collectors

☐ Insurance companies (health, life, property insurance screening)

☐   Communications and utility companies (e.g., mobile phone; pay TV, electric, gas, water)

☐   Retail stores for product return fraud and abuse screening; as well as retail stores that offer financing such as appliance and rent-to-own businesses, among others

☐   Gaming casinos that extend credit to consumers and/or accept personal checks

You can get rejected without warning

With the exception of employment screening, users of consumer reports generally do not warn you in advance if they are about to take an adverse action against you based in whole or in part on your consumer report. Outside of employment screening, adverse action notifications are provided after the fact, say, when you have already been rejected for a home loan, residential rental property or auto lease. The accuracy and completeness of your consumer reporting data, therefore, (as you can see) is extremely important.

The good news is you have a meaningful role to play to ensure your data is accurate and complete. The first step is to request your consumer reports from the consumer reporting companies you think might be important to you. The second step is to review your reports closely. The third step is to dispute suspected inaccuracies as needed. This Introduction describes these steps in detail.

How to request a report

Under the Federal Fair Credit Reporting Act (FCRA), all consumer reporting companies are required to provide you a copy of the information in your report if you request it. Many must do so every twelve months for free upon your request. Additionally, they must give you a free copy of your information if you request it when an adverse action is taken against you based on information in your report from that company and under other specific circumstances. All consumer reporting companies must provide you with a copy of your information for a reasonable fee (for calendar year 2018, the maximum allowable fee is $12.00). Requesting copies of your own consumer reports does not hurt your credit scores. For companies required to provide the information in your report for free annually upon request, they must do so within fifteen days of receiving your request.

Not every consumer reporting company will have information on every consumer. A reporting company that specializes on insurance claim data, for example, will likely not have information about you if you have never filed an insurance claim. Also, some consumers with limited and/or out-of-date credit histories (sometimes known as "credit invisibles") may not have enough information for credit reporting companies to have reports about them. You may be one of those consumers, although if you are making purchases using credit, or if you have credit that is delinquent and is being reported on to your credit reports by a debt collector, it's unlikely. According to FCRA research, consumers in lower-income areas are more likely than those in higher-income areas to become newly credit visible due to negative credit report records such as a debt in collection.

You can get your report from most of the companies in this list for free

Most of the companies in this list will provide your information to you for free. We tell you which do. A few companies in the list will also provide you with a free risk score too if you request it. We tell you which of those do as well. To order your report from a company listed below, click on the company link we provide. Some companies have separate forms for requests by postal mail. We provide links to those forms for you.

Complete contact numbers, address and phone numbers for the big three (Equifax, Experian and TransUnion) are listed below in the "How to Get a Copy of Your Credit Reports" narrative.

Know when to check a report

It's important to fact-check your credit reports from the three nationwide consumer reporting companies (Equifax, Experian, TransUnion) every twelve months to ensure they are accurate and complete, especially if you intend to purchase a home or car with credit, or otherwise intend to apply for credit in the future. Roughly 90% of consumers with credit files aren't taking advantage of the free benefit to request their credit reports.

There isn't just "one" credit risk score, so it's important to focus on the reporting information itself from which risk scores are derived. If you are applying for a job, lease (home or auto) or insurance policy, also fact-check your background screening reports to ensure there are no errors. You are given detailed tips on when best to check those reports in the sections below as appropriate.

Finally, if you have been, or fear you may become, a victim of identity theft, fact-check your reports. Data breaches are an unfortunate reality. It's important to be aware of your options to take greater control of your consumer reporting data. In this year's edition of this report, pointed out is which company websites have additional information for you about your options to block access to your consumer reporting data for certain purposes through a security "freeze," subject to the laws in the state where you reside and also attendant applicable fees.

You have the right to dispute the information in your reports

If you find information in your consumer report that you believe is inaccurate or incomplete, you have the legal right to dispute the report's content with the consumer reporting company <u>and the company</u> that shared the information to the reporting company, such as your lender.

Under the FCRA, companies must conduct – free of charge – a reasonable investigation of your dispute. The company that has provided the incorrect information must correct the error and notify all of the consumer reporting companies to whom it provided the inaccurate information.

See Consumer Financial Protection Bureau, Consumer Voices on Credit Reports and Scores, (Feb. 2015), available at https://www.consumerfinance.gov/data-research/research-reports/consumer-voices-on-credit-reports-and-scores .

Of course, **if your information is current and accurate, even if negative,** you will not be able to remove it. Some may claim that they can remove negative information, but if the information in your report is accurate and current – beware! – it's probably a credit repair scam.

You can learn more about disputing a reporting error on the FCRA website, and what to do if you see the same error in more than one report. You can also submit a complaint to FCRA. They will forward your complaint to the company and work to get you a response.

The FCRA is there if you have complaints about your consumer reports.

They handle consumer reporting complaints about report accuracy and completeness errors and other consumer reporting topics, such as, if you are dissatisfied with a company's investigation of an earlier dispute, if you believe your consumer report was used improperly, if you have problems getting access to your own consumer reports, or if you are dissatisfied with consumer reporting products and services provided to you, such as credit monitoring and identity protection services. The FCRA also handles complaints about credit repair. They help consumers connect with financial companies to understand issues, fix errors, and get direct responses about problems.

Listing of Consumer Reporting Companies

Following is a list of consumer reporting companies (by 10 distinct categories) updated for 2018.

Employment screening

Employment screening companies provide verification information such as credit history, employment, salary and education and professional license verification to employers and others. They may also provide criminal arrest and conviction information as well as fingerprint information from state and federal criminal record databases; driving record information; drug and alcohol testing and health screening information; and non-profit and volunteer activity verification.

Many employment screening companies won't have information on you unless you authorized an employer or other end-user to obtain a report. If possible, when you give your authorization, ask for the name(s) of the employment screening company being used. Contact those reporting companies to fact-check your reports. If the employer is checking your credit history in separate reports, from one or all three of the nationwide providers of consumer reports listed above, request and review those reports too.

Accurate Background	
Website https://accuratebackground.com	**Phone** 800-216-8024
Provides background screening services. The company will provide one free report if you request it.	**Address** Accurate Background, Inc. Dispute Department 7515 Irvine Center Drive Irvine, CA 92618

American DataBank	
Website http://Americandatabank.com	**Phone** 800-200-0853
Provides background screening services. The company will provide one free report every 12 months if you request it.	**Address** American DataBank 110 Sixteenth Street, 8th Floor Denver, CO 80202

backgroundchecks.com	
Website http://backgroundchecks.com	**Phone** 866-265-6602
Provides background screening services. backgroundchecks.com is affiliated with General Information Services, Inc. (GIS)	**Address** backgroundchecks.com Attn: consumer relations department P.O. Box 353 Chapin, SC 29036

Checkr	
Website http://checkr.com	**Phone – n/a** **Email** hello@checkr.com
Provides background screening services. The company allows consumers to review their reports via its Applicant Portal only at https://applicant.checkr.com/	**Address** One Montgomery Street, Suite 2000 San Francisco, CA 94108

First Advantage Corporation	
Website http://FADV.com	**Phone** 800.845.6004
Provides background screening services. The company will provide one free report every 12 months if you request it. **Freeze your report:** The company will freeze your consumer report (subject to state laws) if you request it.	**Address** First Advantage Consumer Center P.O. Box 105292 Atlanta, GA 30348-5292

General Information Services, Inc. (GIS)	
Website http://GenInfo.com	**Phone** 866-265-4917
Provides background screening services. The company will provide one free report every 12 months if you request it.	**Address** General Information Services Attn: consumer relations department P.O. Box 353 Chapin, SC 29036

HireRight	
Website http://HireRight.com	**Phone** 866-521-6995 followed by Option 1
Provides background screening services. The company will provide one free report every 12 months if you request it.	**Address** HireRight, LLC Attn: Consumers Department 14002 E. 21st Street, Suite 1200 Tulsa, OK 74134

Info Cubic	
Website *(Report Request)* https://www.infocubic.com/doc/Consumer-Report-Copy-Request.pdf	**Phone** 877-360-4636
Provides background screening services. The company will provide one free report every 12 months if you request it.	**Address** Info Cubic LLC 9250 E. Costilla Ave., Suite 525 Greenwood Village, CO 80112

OPENonline	
Website (Report Request) https://services.openonline.com /Pages/Compliance/ RequestInformation.aspx	**Phone** 888-381-5656
Provides background screening services. The company will provide one free report every 12 months if you request it.	**Address** OPENonline, LLC Attn: Compliance PO Box 549 Columbus, OH 43216-0549

Pre-employ.com	
Website http://www.Pre-employ.com	**Phone** 800-300-1821 (extension 199)
Provides background screening services. The company will provide one free report every 12 months if you request it.	**Address** Pre-employ PO Box 491570 Redding, CA 96049

Sterling Talent Solutions

Website	Phone
https://www.sterlingtalentsolutions.com	888-889-5248 (Option 3 followed by Option 2)
Provides background screening services. The company will provide one free report every 12 months if you request it.	**Address** Sterling Talent Solutions ATTN: Consumer Reports 4511 Rockside Road Independence, OH 44131

Trak 1

Website (Report Request)	Phone
https://trak-1.com/wp-content/uploads/2013/03/Consumer-Report-Request-Form1.pdf	918-779-7000
Provides background screening services. The company will provide one free report every 12 months if you request it.	**Address** Trak-1 Consumer Report Request 7131 Riverside Parkway Tulsa, OK 74136

IntelliCorp

Website	Phone
Pending ?	866-202-1436
Provides background screening services. IntelliCorp is a subsidiary of Verisk Analytics. The company will provide one free report every 12 months if you request it.	**Address** IntelliCorp Records, Inc. 3000 Auburn Drive, Suite 410 Beachwood, OH 44122

The Work Number

Provides employment and income information. It includes data collected from employers and large private sector payroll processors. The Work Number provides this information to employers. It also provides this information to government agency clients to determine, for example, an applicant's social service eligibility, or, say, to inform child support collections and enforcement. Equifax Workforce Solutions, also known as TALX Corporation, operates The Work Number. TALX is a wholly owned subsidiary of Equifax. The company will provide one free report every 12 months if you request it.	**Phone** 866-604-6570 (Option 1) **Website** https://www.TheWorkNumber.com **Address** Equifax Workforce Solutions ATTN: EDR 3470 Rider Trail South Suite 337 Earth City, MO 63045

Tenant screening

That's right, there are also specialty consumer reporting agencies that compile information just for landlords to help them decide who they rent to. These agencies collect information such as your name, previous addresses, amount of time at each residence, and payment history records from your past landlords.

If you are applying as a tenant for a residential property, you may want to ask the management company whether it will be pulling your consumer report(s). If the answer is yes, ask for the consumer reporting company name(s). Contact those companies to fact-check those reports and dispute them as needed. A tenant screening report with negative information in it, such as prior evictions, could result in a rejected lease application, or it may get approved but with tough conditions inserted into the lease agreement such as requiring you to pay twelve months of rent in advance of your move-in date. As such, if you can, consider holding off on submitting your application until you can fact-check your reports and dispute suspected inaccuracies as needed. If the landlord is checking your credit history from one or all three of the nationwide providers of consumer reports listed above, request and review those reports too.

Contemporary Information Corp. (CIC)	
Conducts background screening services for landlords and residential real estate management companies. Information includes eviction and criminal background data. The company will provide one free report pertaining to their national eviction record database every 12 months if you request it.	**Website** http://www.CICreports.com **Phone** 800-288-4757 (Option 5) **Address** CIC Reports Consumer Relations 42913 Capital Drive, Unit 101 Lancaster, CA 93535

CoreLogic Rental Property Solutions

Collects and reports comprehensive information about landlord-tenant actions (such as prior evictions), address history, public background check (to identify prior criminal and court judgments, including prior prison sentences, presence on government-managed sex offender and known terrorist databases).

The company will provide one free report every 12 months if you request it.

Website (Report Request)
https://www.corelogic.com/downloadable-docs/saferent-consumer-disclosure.pdf

Phone
888-333-2413 (Option 1)

Address
CoreLogic Rental Property Solutions, LLC Consumer Relations Department P.O. Box 509124 San Diego, CA 92150

Home Page

https://rental.corelogic.com/rsn/login.aspx

Experian Rent Bureau

Collects rent payment history data from property owners and residential real estate managers, electronic rent payment services and collection companies, and makes that information available to the multifamily housing industry through tenant screening reporting companies. Experian also includes some positive rent data it receives from Experian RentBureau in its standard credit reports. Positive rent data refers to payments that are paid

Website (Report Request)
http://www.experian.com/assets/rentbureau/general/request_form.pdf

Phone
877-704-4519

Address
Experian RentBureau P.O. Box 26 Allen, TX 75013

as agreed between tenants and landlords.	The company will provide one free report every 12 months if you request it.

First Advantage Corporation Resident History Report	
Provides background screening services. **Freeze your report:** The company will freeze your consumer report (subject to state laws) if you request it. The company will provide one free report every 12 months if you request it. You may obtain a copy of your First Advantage consumer file disclosure in one of three ways: 1. Call our toll-free number: 800.845.6004 2. Fax request to 727.214.2127 3. E-mail at consumer.documents@fadv.com	**Website** FADV.com Request report form **Phone** 800-845-6004 **Address** First Advantage Consumer Center P.O. Box 105292 Atlanta, GA 30348-5292

Leasing Desk (Real Page, Inc.)	
Provides data for tenant screening. **Free report:** The company will provide one free report every 12 months if you request it. **Freeze your report:**	**Website** http://www.RealPage.com **Phone** N/A **Address** Real Page, Inc. LeasingDesk Screening Consumer Relations 2201 Lakeside Blvd. Richardson, TX 75082

The company will freeze your consumer report (subject to state laws) if you request it.	

Screening Reports, Inc.

Provides background screening services to the multifamily housing industry. Offers screening services for affordable, conventional and student housing properties. Services consist of previous rental verification and employment verification, consumer credit reports, landlord tenant eviction reports, criminal reports, sex offender reports, and foreign asset compliance (OFAC search). The company will provide one free report every 12 months if you request it.	**Website** http://www.ScreeningReports.com **Phone** 866-389-4042 **Address** Screening Reports, Inc. 220 Gerry Drive Wood Dale, IL 60191

Tenant Data Services

Collects and provides rental performance history such as data on damages, unauthorized pets, lease violations and missed payments. The company will provide one free report every 12 months if you request it.	**Website** (Report Request) http://tenantdata.com/for-consumers/your_personal_report. Html **Phone** 800-228-1837 (Option 6)

	Address
	Personal Report Request Tenant Data Services, Inc. P.O. Box 5404 Lincoln, NE 68505-0404

TransUnion Rental Screening Solutions

Collects and provides tenant screening and verification data for independent landlords and residential real estate management companies. The company will provide one free report every 12 months if you request it. **Website** https://www.mysmartmove.com	**Phone** 888-387-1750 (Option 4) or 866-775-0961 (Option 4) **Address** TransUnion Rental Screening Solutions, Inc. Attn: Escalations Dept. 6430 South Fiddlers Green Circle, Suite 500 Greenwood Village, CO 80111

Check and Bank Screening

Checking account reporting companies do collect and report on information related to your checking account.

These companies, which include Chex Systems and Early Warning Services, collect and report information about checking accounts you've had in the past. If you've had your account closed due to an unpaid negative balance, the bank or credit union would typically report this "involuntary closure" to a checking account reporting company. You may also be reported if you were suspected of fraudulent activity by the bank or credit union. Banks and credit unions often use reports from these companies to help decide whether to offer you a checking account and the type of checking account to offer you.

If you have been a victim of bank and/or check writing fraud, or have had prior difficulties opening or closing a bank account (such as being denied an account), review your check and bank screening report(s) and dispute them if inaccurate. This applies especially if you are about to open a new bank and/or checking account.

Certegy Check Services	
Collects check writing histories and provides check screening services primarily for retail merchants and gaming establishments who accept checks as payment. Certegy is affiliated with Fidelity National Information Services, Inc. (FNIS). The company will provide one free report every 12 months if you request it.	**Website** https://www.AskCertegy.com **Phone** 800-237-3826 **Address** Certegy Check Services Inc. Attn: CFDR Request P.O. Box 30046 Tampa, FL 33630-3296

Cross Check, Inc.

Provides check verification and guarantee services primarily for automotive sales and repair, building supply, home improvement, retail, medical, dental, and veterinarian industries. The company will provide one free report every 12 months if you request it.	**Website** http://www.cross-check.com/consumers-check-writers **Phone** 800-843-0760 **Address** Attn: Consumer Inquiry Department PO Box 6008 Petaluma, CA 94955-6008

ChexSystems

Provides account verification services primarily for financial institutions. Collects and reports data on checking account applications, openings, and closures, including reasons for account closure. When you apply for a new checking account many banks and credit unions will refer to this database to help inform whether to approve your new account. ChexSystems is affiliated with Fidelity National Information Services, Inc. (FNIS). The company will provide one free report every 12 months if you request it. A free score will be provided upon request too.	**Website** ConsumerDebit.com Request report form Request score form Security freeze information Security freeze form **Phone** 800-428-9623 **Address** ChexSystems, Inc. Attn: Consumer Relations 7805 Hudson Road, Suite 100 Woodbury, MN 55125 The company will freeze your consumer report (subject to state laws) if you request it.

Global Payments Check Services, Inc.

Provides check screening and verification services for various consumer-facing industries. The company will provide one free report every 12 months if you request it. **Website** https://www.globalpaymentsinc.com/en-us/customer-center/customer-support/facta	**Phone** 800-638-4600, x410 **Address** Global Payments Check Services, Inc. Attn: FACT ACT Support PO Box 59371 Chicago, IL 60659

Early Warning Services

Assists financial institutions, check acceptance companies such as retail merchants, payment processors and other financial entities in detecting and preventing fraud associated with bank accounts and payment transactions. Early Warning is co-owned by Bank of America, BB&T, Capital One, JPMorgan Chase, PNC Bank, U.S. Bank and Wells Fargo. The company will provide one free report every 12 months if you request it. The company will also provide a deposit risk score if you request it.	**Website** http://www.earlywarning.com/consumer-information.html **Phone** 800-325-7775 (Option 2) **Address** Early Warning Services, LLC Attn: Consumer Services Department 16552 North 90th Street Scottsdale, AZ 85260

Tele Check Services

Assists retailers, financial institutions and other businesses in reducing fraud and other risks associated with accepting payments and opening accounts using check writing, and other checking account related information. TeleCheck is a wholly owned subsidiary of First Data Corporation. The company will provide one free report every 12 months if you request it.	**Website** (Report Request) https://getassistance.telecheck.com/consumer-file-report.html **Phone** 800-366-2425 **Address** Telecheck Services, Inc. Attn: Resolutions Department-FA P.O Box 4514 Houston, TX 77210-4514

Personal Property Insurance

There are specialty consumer reporting agencies that collect information about the insurance claims you have made on your property and casualty insurance policies, such as your homeowners and auto policies. They may also collect driving records. Insurance companies use information in these reports to choose the types of policies they offer you and the premiums you pay.

Fact-check your specialty insurance report before applying for insurance.

A-PLUS Property (by Verisk)	
Collects and reports insurance claims and loss information data associated with homes or commercial buildings. A-PLUS Property is a subsidiary of Verisk Analytics, Inc. The company will provide one free report every 12 months if you request it.	**Website** https://www.verisk.com/insurance/products/order-an-a-plus-loss-history-report/ **Phone** 800-627-3487 (Option 2) **Address** A-PLUS Consumer Inquiry Center 545 Washington Boulevard, FL 22 Jersey City, NJ 07310-1686

C.L.U.E. Inc. (Personal Property & Auto Reports)	
C.L.U.E. (Comprehensive Loss Underwriting Exchange) collects and reports information on insurance coverage, losses associated with individuals and their personal property, as well as automobile insurance coverage and losses. C.L.U.E. Inc. is affiliated with LexisNexis Risk Solutions.	**Website** https://personalreports.lexisnexis.com/fact_act_disclosure.jsp **Phone** 866-312-8076 **Address** C.L.U.E. Inc. Consumer Center P.O. Box 105295 Atlanta, GA 30348-5295

The company will provide one free report every 12 months if you request it	

Drivers History

Provides reports to its insurance clients containing information and data collected from open public sources and governmental agencies regarding driving violations issued to specific individuals. TransUnion has a majority ownership interest in Drivers History.	**Website** http://DriversHistory.com **Phone** 855-694-1555 **Address** Drivers History Consumer Relations P.O. Box 600 Woodlyn, PA 19094

Insurance Information Exchange (iiX)

Collects and reports motor vehicle records, including traffic violation data to insurance providers and prospective employers. The company also provides employment and education verification services. Insurance Information Exchange is a subsidiary of Verisk Analytics, Inc. The company will provide one free report every 12 months if you request it.	**Website** (Report Request) https://www.verisk.com/siteassets/iix/downloads/fcrarelease.pdf **Phone** 866-560-7015 **Address** iiX Attn: Valerie Coones 1716 Briarcrest Drive, Suite 200 Bryan, TX 77802

Medical

These agencies may supply reports on your prescription drug purchase histories, medical conditions, data from your insurance applications, and data from other sources. Life insurance companies, for example, commonly use these reports to evaluate policy applications from potential customers.

Fact-check your medical specialty report before applying for private life, health, critical illness, long-term care or disability income insurance.

MIB, Inc.	
Collects information about medical conditions and hazardous avocations with your authorization. It reports this information to life and health insurance companies to assess your risk and eligibility during the underwriting of individual (rather than as a member of a group) life, health, disability income, critical illness, and long-term care insurance policies. Generally, you will not have an MIB consumer report unless you applied for individually underwritten life or health insurance at an MIB member insurance company within the past seven years.	**Website** (Report Request) http://www.mib.com/facts_about_mib.html **Phone** 866-692-6901 **Address** MIB, Inc. 50 Braintree Hill Park, Suite 400 Braintree, MA 02184-8734 MIB, Inc. is a subsidiary of MIB Group, Inc. The company will provide one free report every 12 months if you request it.

Milliman Intelli Script	
Collects information on your prescription drug purchase history. You may have a prescription report about you if you authorized the release of your medical records to an insurance company and that company submitted a request to Milliman.	**Website** (Report Request) http://www.rxhistories.com/RequestAReport/ **Phone** 877-211-4816 **Address** Milliman IntelliScript 15800 W. Bluemound Road, Suite 100 Brookfield, WI 53005

Low-income and Subprime

Clarity Services	
Collects and provides information on payday loans, installment loans, auto loans (and leasing), check cashing services, rent-to-own transactions, telecommunication account openings, and financial services with an emphasis on the lower-income and subprime consumer market segments. Clarity Services is owned by Experian. The company will provide one free report every 12 months if you request it. The company will also provide a credit risk score if you request it	**Website** (Report Request) https://www.clarityservices.com/wp-content/uploads/2016/08/File-Disclosure-Request-08-23-16.pdf **Phone** 866-390-3118 (Option 1 for security freeze; Option 4 for report request). **Address** Clarity Services, Inc. P.O. Box 5717 Clearwater, FL 33758 The company will freeze your consumer report (subject to state laws) if you request it.

DataX

Collects and provides payment history regarding subprime consumers. The company will provide one free report every 12 months if you request it. **Website** (Request Form) http://consumers.dataxltd.com/	**Phone** 800-295-4790 (Option 3) **Address** Data X, Ltd. Attn: Customer Service 325 E. Warm Springs Road, Suite 202 Attn: Customer Service Las Vegas, NV 89119

CoreLogic Tele track

Collects consumer information about, and provides data to, payday lenders, rent-to-own businesses, furniture stores that offer financing, auto finance and leasing companies, high risk consumer finance businesses, subprime home lending businesses, subprime credit card issuers, banks, credit unions, cable/telecom companies and debt buyers/collectors. The company will provide one free report every 12 months if you request it.	**Website (Report Request)** https://www.corelogic.com/solutions/teletrack-consumer-assistance.aspx **Phone** 877-309-5226 **Address** CoreLogic Teletrack P.O. Box 509124 San Diego, CA 92150 Attention: Consumer Disputes Department Teletrack is affiliated with CoreLogic.

FactorTrust

Collects loan performance information on nonprime consumers to provide predictive credit data, analytics and risk scoring solutions to short-term lenders, installment lenders, nonprime auto lenders (and leasing companies) and other subprime credit providers. The company will provide one free report every 12 months if you request it. The company will freeze your consumer report (subject to state laws) if you request it.	**Website** (Report Request) https://www.factortrust.com/consumer/ ReportRequest.aspx **Phone** 844-773-3321 **Address** FactorTrust, Inc. Attn: Consumer Inquiries P.O. Box 3653 Alpharetta, GA 30023 FactorTrust is owned by TransUnion.

MicroBilt / PRBC

Provides consumer credit information, bill payment information, employment information, bank account data, property records, court judgments, address and phone information on low-income and subprime consumers to businesses that offer short term, rent-to-own, auto, retail and consumer finance lending. The company will provide one free report every 12 months if you request it. Upon request, a free score, if available, will be provided with the report	**Website** (Report Request) http://www.microbilt.com/ **Phone** 888-222-7621 **Address** MicroBilt / PRBC Attn: Consumer Affairs Department P.O. Box 440693 Kennesaw, GA 30160 The company will freeze your consumer report (subject to state laws) if you request it.

Supplementary Reports

CoreLogic Credco	
Collects and reports personal data such as property ownership and home loan obligation records; property legal filings and tax payment status; rental applications and collection accounts; consumer bankruptcies, liens, judgments, and child support obligations. The company will provide one free report every 12 months if you request it. The company will freeze your consumer report (subject to state laws) if you request it.	**Website** (Report Request) https://www.corelogic.com/solutions/credco-consumer-assistance.aspx **Phone** 877-532-8778 (CoreLogic Credco Consumer File inquiries) **Address** CoreLogic Credco, LLC P.O. Box 509124 San Diego, CA 92150

Innovis	
Provides ID verification data to assist with fraud detection and prevention. The company will provide one free report every 12 months if you request it. The company will freeze your consumer report (subject to state laws) if you request it.	**Website** (Report Request) https://www.innovis.com/personal/creditReport **Phone** 800-540-2505 **Address** Innovis Consumer Assistance P.O. Box 1640 Pittsburgh, PA 15230-1640

LexisNexis Risk Solutions

Collects information from public records and multiple proprietary data sources. This includes items such as real estate transaction and ownership data, lien, judgment, and bankruptcy records, professional license information, and historical addresses on file.

The company will provide one free report every 12 months if you request it.

The company will freeze your consumer report (subject to state laws) if you request it.

Website (Report Request)
https://personalreports.lexisnexis.com/pdfs/CD107_CP-File-Disclosure-Request-Form_pg-3.pdf

Phone
866-897-8126

Address
LexisNexis Consumer Center Attn: Full File Disclosure P.O. Box 105108 Atlanta, GA 30348-5108

SageStream (subsidiary of ID Analytics, LLC)

This reporting company collects information from, and provides supplementary consumer reports to, auto lenders, credit card issuers, retailers, utilities and mobile phone service providers among other service providers.

The company will provide one free report every 12 months if you request it.

The company will freeze your consumer report (subject to state laws) if you request it.

Website (Report Request)
https://www.sagestreamllc.com/security-freeze/

Phone
888-395-0277 (Option 1)

Address
SageStream, LLC
Consumer Office
P.O. Box 503793
San Diego, CA 92150

Utilities

National Consumer Telecommunications & Utilities Exchange	
Collects information on new telecom and utility connect requests, account and payment histories, defaults, and fraudulent accounts associated with telecommunications, pay TV, and utility (electric, gas, water) services to help companies in the telecommunications and utility industries identify high risk consumers. The company will provide one free report every 12 months if you request it. The company will freeze your consumer report (subject to state laws) if you request it.	**Website** (Report Request) http://www.nctue.com/Consumers **Phone** 866-349-5185 (Option 1) **Address** NCTUE Disclosure Report P.O. Box 105161 Atlanta, GA 30348 NCTUE Security Freeze P.O. Box 105561 Atlanta, GA 30348

Retail

The Retail Equation	
Monitors and reports to merchant's retail product return and exchange fraud and abuse.	**Website** (Report Request) https://www.theretailequation.com/Consumers/ReturnActivityReport.aspx **Phone** 800-652-2331 **Address** The Retail Equation P.O. Box 51373 Irvine, CA 92619-1373

Gaming

VIP Preferred	
Provides consumer data to assist casinos and other gaming establishments such as racetracks to manage the risk associated with check cashing settlement services to consumers. The company will provide one free report every 12 months if you request it.	**Website** (Report Request) https://www.vippreferred.com/en/facta-report **Phone** 800-638-4600, x410 **Address** Global Payments Gaming Services, Inc. Attn: FACT ACT Support PO Box 59371 Chicago, IL 60659

Building Credit from Scratch

Starting out in the financial world can be confusing. And building good credit takes time. Below are some types of helpful products, as well as actions you can take to help reach your financial goals.

Finding the right products

Secured credit cards

Apply for this card as you would a traditional credit card. Once approved you deposit an amount of money –which can range from $50 to $300– into a separate account. The bank holds onto this deposit and extends a credit line matching the deposit amount. Generally, you can build credit with a secured card, but be sure to ask your card issuer about reporting to the credit reporting companies. Many of these cards include a "graduation" component, so you are able to move from a secured card to a traditional credit card seamlessly after establishing a pattern of consistent payments.

Credit builder loans

Financial institutions, typically credit unions, deposit a small "loan" (often $300-$1000) into a locked savings account and then you pay the institution back with small-dollar payments over 6 to 24 months. These payments are reported to the credit reporting companies. Once you come to the end of the loan term, you receive the accumulated money back in total.

Know what matters

Paying your credit card bills or other loan payments on time is one critical step in building a good credit score. Also, don't get too close to the credit limit.

Credit scoring models look at how close you are to being "maxed out." Formulas predict that people who use too much of their available credit may have future troubles with repayment. Experts advise keeping use at no more than 30% of your total credit limit. Credit scores may also decline if you apply for and open too many credit accounts, such as credit cards, in a short time.

Take steps to correct errors

You should actively take steps to correct any issues with your credit report. After accessing your report, you will have a better understanding of your current creditworthiness and be able to request an investigation of any errors or inaccuracies you find.

Retail Store Cards

Many gas stations, department stores or retail chains offer credit cards. These cards tend to be easier to obtain and typically offer lower credit lines. This combination makes them an option when you are looking to build up a thin or nonexistent credit record.

Actions you can take & things to know about your credit report and score

Get and read your credit report

The first and most important step in building and maintaining good credit is to know and understand what is in your credit report. You are entitled to and can request your credit report from each of the three nationwide credit reporting companies once every 12 months free of charge at annualcreditreport.com.

How to Get a Copy of Your Credit Reports

You are entitled to a free credit report every 12 months from each of the three major consumer reporting companies (Equifax, Experian and TransUnion). You can request a copy from AnnualCreditReport.com.

You can request and review your free report through one of the following ways:

- **Online**: Visit AnnualCreditReport.com
- **Phone**: Call 1-877-322-8228
- **Mail**: Download and complete the Annual Credit Report Request form. Mail the completed form to:

Annual Credit Report Request Service
P.O. Box 105281
Atlanta, GA 30348-5281

You can request all three reports at once or you can order one report at a time. By requesting the reports separately (for example, one every four months) you can monitor your credit report throughout the year. Once you've received your annual free credit report, you can still request additional reports. By law, a credit reporting company can charge no more than $12.00 for a credit report.

You are also eligible for reports from specialty consumer reporting companies. We put together a list of several of these companies so you can see which ones might be important to you. You have to request the reports individually from each of these companies. Many of the companies in this list will provide a report for free every 12 months. Other companies may charge you a fee for your report.

You can get additional free reports if any of the following apply to you:

- You received a notice that you were denied credit, insurance, or employment or experienced another "adverse action" based on a credit report, you have a right to a free report from the credit reporting company identified in the notice. To get the free report you must request it within 60 days after you receive the notice. Other types of "adverse action" notices you might receive include notice of an unfavorable change in the terms or amount of your credit or insurance

coverage, or unfavorable changes in the terms of your employment or of a license or other government benefit.
- You believe your file is inaccurate due to fraud.
- You have requested a credit report from a nationwide credit reporting company in connection with the placing of an initial fraud alert (you may request two free copies for an extended fraud alert).
- You are unemployed and intend to apply for employment within 60 days from the date of your request.
- You are a recipient of public welfare assistance.
- Your state law provides for a free credit report.

Tip:

Be cautious of websites that claim to offer free credit reports. Some of these websites will only give you a free report if you buy other products or services. Other websites give you a free report and then bill you for services you have to cancel. To get the free credit report authorized by law, go to AnnualCreditReport.com or call (877) 322-8228.

The **Consumer Financial Protection Bureau** (CFPB) is a U.S. government agency that makes sure banks, lenders, and other financial companies treat you fairly.

Whether you have questions about the CFPB or about a consumer financial product or service, or you want to submit a complaint, start here. They will point you in the right direction.

Phone (855) 411-CFPB 411-2372 TTY/TDD 729-CFPB (855) 729-2372 8 am-8 pm Monday through Friday More than 180 languages available	**Fax** (855) 237-2392
Mailing address Consumer Financial Protection Bureau	**Headquarters address** Consumer Financial Protection Bureau

PO Box 2900 Clinton, IA 52733-2900	1700 G St. N.W. Washington, D.C. 20552
Online https://www.consumerfinance.gov/	Consumer Financial Protection Bureau 1990 K St. N.W. Washington, D.C. 20006

Submit a complaint

There are five steps to submit your complaint:

Step 1: What is this complaint about?

Step 2: What type of problem are you having?

Step 3: What happened?

Step 4: What company is this complaint about?

Step 5: Who are the people involved?

Before you get started

You'll need the dates, amounts, and other details about your complaint. If you have documents you want to include, such as billing statements or letters from the company, you'll be able to attach them in Step 3.

Make sure to include all the information you can, because you generally can't submit a second complaint about the same problem.

We'll forward your complaint and any documents you provide to the company and work to get you a response – generally within 15 days.

Visit the Consumer Financial Protection Bureau here to document your complaint; https://www.consumerfinance.gov/complaint/getting-started/

Frequently Asked Questions

Please realize that the content in the FAQ page provides general consumer information. It is not legal advice or regulatory guidance. This information may include links or references to third-party resources or content. I do not endorse the third-party or guarantee the accuracy of any third-party information. There may be other resources that also serve your needs.

Will requesting my credit report hurt my credit score?

Answer: No, requesting your credit report will not hurt your credit score.

Checking your own credit report is not an inquiry about new credit, so it has no effect on your score. In fact, reviewing your credit report regularly can help you to ensure that the information the credit reporting companies share with lenders is accurate and up-to-date.

You are entitled to a free credit report every 12 months from each of the three major consumer reporting companies (Equifax, Experian and TransUnion).

How do I dispute an error on my credit report?

Answer: To dispute an error on your credit report, contact both the credit reporting company and the company that provided the information.

Step 1: Dispute the information with the credit reporting company.

If you identify an error on your credit report, you should start by disputing that information with the credit reporting company (Experian, Equifax, and/or Transunion).You should explain in writing what you think is wrong, why, and include copies of documents that support your dispute. You can also use our instructions and template letter as a guide.

If you mail a dispute, your dispute letter should include:

- Contact information for you including complete name, address, and telephone number
- Report confirmation number, if available
- Clearly identify each mistake, such as an account number for any account you may be disputing

- Explain why you are disputing the information
- Request that the information be removed or corrected
- Enclose a copy of the portion of your credit report that contains the disputed items and circle or highlight the disputed items. You should include copies (not originals) of documents that support your position.

You may choose to send your letter of dispute to credit reporting companies by certified mail and ask for a return receipt, so that you will have a record that your letter was received.

You can contact the nationwide credit reporting companies online, by mail, or by phone:

Equifax

Online: www.ai.equifax.com/CreditInvestigation

By mail: Download the dispute form
Mail the dispute form with your letter to:

Equifax Information Services LLC
P.O. Box 740256
Atlanta, GA 30348

By phone: Phone number provided on credit report or (866) 349-5191

Experian

Online: www.experian.com/disputes/main.html

By mail: Use the address provided on your credit report or mail your letter to:

Experian
P.O. Box 4500
Allen, TX 75013

By phone: Phone number provided on credit report or (888) 397-3742

TransUnion

Online: https://dispute.transunion.com

By mail: Download the dispute form
Mail the dispute form with your letter to:

TransUnion LLC
Consumer Dispute Center
P.O. Box 2000
Chester, PA 19016

By phone: (800) 916-8800

Keep copies of your dispute letter and enclosures.

Step 2: Dispute the information with the company who provided the information (also known as the furnisher).

If you would like to submit a dispute regarding the information a company provided to the credit reporting company (called a furnisher), use our instructions, along with a template letter as a guide. Examples of information furnishers are your bank, your apartment landlord or your credit card company.

What happens after you dispute information on your credit report?

Credit reporting companies must investigate your dispute, forward all documents to the furnisher, and report the results back to you unless they determine your claim is frivolous. If the consumer reporting company or furnisher determines that your dispute is frivolous, it can choose not to investigate the dispute so long as it sends you a notice within five days saying that it has made such a determination.

If the furnisher corrects your information after your dispute, it must notify all of the credit reporting companies it sent the inaccurate information to, so they can update their reports with the correct information.

If the furnisher determines that the information is accurate and does not update or remove the information, you can request the credit reporting company to include a statement explaining the dispute in your credit file. This statement will be included in future reports and provided to whoever requests your credit report.

Tip: If you suspect that the error on your report is a result of identity theft, visit IdentityTheft.gov, the federal government's one-stop resource to help you report and recover from identity theft.

What are specialty consumer reporting agencies and what kind of information do they collect?

Answer: Specialty consumer reporting companies collect and share information about your employment history, transaction history with a business or repayment history for a specific product or service.

The information specialty consumer reporting companies collect depends on the reporting company and its specialty industry.

Reports may be compiled from your history of:

- Opening or using bank accounts (including bounced checks or overdrafts)
- Apartment rental payments
- Car insurance claims
- Homeowners and renters insurance claims
- Employment
- Medical records or payments

You might not know these reports exist unless you run into a problem, such as not getting a job, lease, insurance, or checking account, or when a utility or cell phone company asks you to put down a deposit before starting service with you.

Just like with the big three consumer reporting companies, you can get free copies of your reports every 12 months from many of the specialty consumer reporting companies. Other specialty consumer reporting companies may be able to charge you a fee for your report. Keep in mind that not every consumer reporting company will have information on everyone. You have to request the reports individually from each company.

What do I do if I think I have been a victim of identity theft?

Answer: If you think you've been a victim of fraud or identity theft, contact one of the nationwide credit reporting companies and place a fraud alert in your credit report.

You can contact the three nationwide credit reporting companies, Equifax, Experian, and TransUnion:

Online	By calling	By mail
Equifax Alerts	(888) 766-0008	Equifax Consumer Fraud Division, PO Box 740256, Atlanta, GA 30374
Experian Fraud Center	(888) 397-3742	Experian, P.O. Box 9554, Allen, TX 75013
Transunion Fraud Alert	(888) 909-8872	TransUnion Fraud Victim Assistance Department, P.O. Box 2000, Chester, PA 19016

A fraud alert requires creditors who check your credit report to take steps to verify your identity before opening a new account, issuing an additional card, or increasing the credit limit on an existing account based on a consumer's request. When you place a fraud alert on your credit report at one of the nationwide credit reporting companies, it must notify the others.

There are two main types of fraud alerts: initial fraud alerts and extended alerts.

Initial fraud alerts

You can place an initial fraud alert on your credit report if you believe you are (or are about to become), a victim of fraud or identity theft. Credit reporting companies will keep that alert on your file for 90 days. After 90 days the initial fraud alert will expire and be removed, you have the option to place another initial fraud alert at that time. An initial fraud alert requires that the creditor take reasonable steps to make sure the person making a new credit request in your name is actually you. If you provide a telephone number, the lender must call you or take reasonable steps to verify whether you are the person making the credit request.

When you place an initial fraud alert in your file, you're entitled to order one free copy of your credit report from each of the nationwide credit reporting companies. These free reports do not count as your free annual report from each credit reporting company.

Extended alerts

You can place an extended alert on your credit report after your identity has been stolen and you file an identity theft report.

When you place an extended fraud alert in your file, you're entitled to order two free copies of your credit report from each nationwide credit reporting company over a 12-month period.

An extended alert is good for seven years. An extended alert requires that the creditor contact you in person or through the telephone number or other contact method you designate to verify whether you are the person making the credit request.

Security freezes

You can also place a "security freeze" on your credit report, which prevents new creditors from accessing your credit file and others from opening accounts in your name, until you lift the freeze.

Unlike fraud alerts, if you place a security freeze with one credit reporting company they will not notify the other credit reporting companies. You must contact each credit reporting company individually if you would like to place a security freeze with all three nationwide credit reporting companies.

Because most businesses will not open credit accounts without checking your credit report, a freeze can stop identity thieves from opening new accounts in your name. Be mindful that a freeze doesn't prevent identity thieves from taking over existing accounts. States have their own rules about credit freezes and how much you pay for them.

Special help for servicemembers

Members of the military (such as members of the Marines, Army, Navy, Air Force, and Coast Guard) have an additional option available to them – active duty alerts, which give service members protection while they are on active duty. Active duty alerts last for 12 months.

When you place an active duty alert on your credit report, creditors must take reasonable steps to make sure the person making the request is actually you before opening an account, issuing an additional credit card on an existing account, or increasing the credit limit on your existing account. Your name also will be removed for two years from the nationwide credit reporting companies' pre-screen marketing lists for credit offers and insurance.

Tip: To file an identity theft report, you must file either a police report or a report with a government agency such as the Federal Trade Commission.

My credit application was denied because of my credit report. What can I do?

Answer: If you were turned down for a loan or a line of credit, the lender is required to give you a list of the main reasons for its decision or a notice telling you how to get the main reasons.

First, find out what caused the lender to turn you down. If a lender rejects your application, it's required under the Equal Credit Opportunity Act (ECOA) to tell you the specific reasons your application was rejected or tell you that you have the right to learn the reasons if you ask within 60 days.

If a lender rejects your application based on your credit report, the lender is also required to:

- Provide you the numerical credit score it used in taking the adverse action and the key factors that affected your score
- Give you the name, address, and telephone number of the credit reporting company that provided the report
- Tell you about your right to get a free copy of your credit report from the credit reporting company that provided it within 60 days of your adverse action notice
- Explain the process for fixing mistakes on your report or adding information to make your report more complete

If you find information in your credit report that you believe is inaccurate, you can dispute what is in the report with the credit reporting company and the company that provided the information. The credit reporting company is required to conduct an investigation and correct any errors it finds. If after the investigation you still believe that the report is wrong, you generally have the right to have a statement added to the report stating that you dispute the information.

If you were denied due to an "insufficient credit file", you can use this checklist to learn how to build and keep good credit.

It is illegal for a creditor to discriminate in any credit transaction, including mortgages, against any applicant because of:

- Race
- Color
- Religion
- National origin
- Sex (gender)
- Marital status
- Age, unless the applicant is not legally able to enter into a contract
- Receipt of income from any public assistance program
- Exercising in good faith a right under the Consumer Credit Protection Act (such as disputing information in your credit report)

If you feel you may have been discriminated against, learn more about your rights under ECOA.

updated JUN 08, 2017

What are common credit report errors that I should look for on my credit report?

Answer: When reviewing your credit report, check that it contains only items about you. Be sure to look for information that is inaccurate or incomplete.

Some common errors in credit reports are:

Identity errors

- Errors made to your identity information (wrong name, phone number, address)
- Accounts belonging to another person with the same or a similar name as yours (this mixing of two consumers' information in a single file is called a mixed file)
- Incorrect accounts resulting from identity theft

Incorrect reporting of account status

- Closed accounts reported as open
- You are reported as the owner of the account, when you are actually just an authorized user
- Accounts that are incorrectly reported as late or delinquent

- Incorrect date of last payment, date opened, or date of first delinquency
- Same debt listed more than once (possibly with different names)

Data management errors

- Reinsertion of incorrect information after it was corrected
- Accounts that appear multiple times with different creditors listed (especially in the case of delinquent accounts or accounts in collections)

Balance Errors

- Accounts with an incorrect current balance
- Accounts with an incorrect credit limit

If you find errors, you should contact the credit reporting company who sent you the report, and the creditor or company that provided the information (called the "furnisher" of the information). Your credit report includes directions about how to dispute inaccurate or incomplete information or you can use our sample dispute letters for furnishers and credit reporting companies.

I've been looking for a job. What do employers see when they do credit checks and background checks?

Answer: Hundreds of companies provide employment background checks and qualify as consumer reporting agencies. Employment reports often include credit checks, criminal background checks, public records – such as bankruptcy filings and other court documents – and information related to your employment history.

An employer needs to get your written permission if it seeks an employment background report on you. If an employer wants to use the information from the report to take an "adverse action" against you, such as not hiring you, it must give you a copy of the report it received beforehand upon request. You will also receive an "adverse action" notice when the employer takes the action against you. The "adverse action" notice will include the name and contact information of the consumer reporting agency from which the employer got the consumer report.

Tip: If an employer wants to use the information from the report to take an "adverse action" against you, such as not hiring you, it must give you a copy of the report it received beforehand. Review your report, and if you spot any errors, you can ask that the errors be corrected.

Just like with the big three consumer reporting agencies, you can get free copies of your reports every 12 months from many of the specialty consumer reporting agencies. Other specialty consumer reporting agencies may be able to charge you a fee for your report. Keep in mind that not every agency will have information on everyone.

What is the difference between a credit report and a credit score?

Answer: Your credit reports and your credit scores are two different things. A credit report is a statement that has information about your credit activity and current credit situation such as loan paying history and the status of your credit accounts. Your credit scores are calculated based on the information in your credit report.

Your credit score, as well as the information on your credit report, are important for determining whether you'll be able to get a mortgage, credit card, auto loan, or other credit product, and the rate you'll pay. Your credit scores are calculated based on the information in your credit report.

You have many different credit scores, and there are many ways to get a credit score. Your score can differ depending on which credit reporting agency provided the information, the scoring model, the type of loan product, and even the day when it was calculated. Higher scores reflect a better loan paying history and make you eligible for lower interest rates.

Errors on your credit report can reduce your score artificially - which could mean a higher interest rate and less money in your pocket - so it is important to check your credit report and correct any errors well before you apply for a loan.

You have many different credit scores

It's normal to see slightly different numbers

EXAMPLE:    EXAMPLE:    EXAMPLE:

You saw your credit score online, provided by your credit card company	You signed up for a separate, free credit monitoring service, and checked your score there	Your auto lender showed you the credit score it used to evaluate your loan application

TIP: At a given point in time, lenders are probably looking at slightly different scores than the ones you see.

Scores are calculated at different times, in different ways

Credit report data   **Timing**   **Scoring models**

Credit report data	Timing	Scoring models
A score uses data from a credit reporting company, and each may have slightly different data: • Equifax • TransUnion • Experian • Others	Your scores are not calculated on a fixed schedule, so they depend on: • When data is updated at a reporting company • When your score is actually calculated	Companies have created multiple versions of their scoring models and update them frequently: • FICO • VantageScore • Other custom models

TIP: Parts of the credit score business are beyond your control. What you can do is make it a habit to check your credit reports each year through annualcreditreport.com and fix any errors.

Your credit history and behavior form the basis of your credit scores

Payment history   **Current unpaid debt**   **Length of credit history**

% of available credit used   **Type of debt and when it started**   **New applications for credit**

TIP: The way you use and repay debt affects your credit score, so your score can be helpful in tracking and improving your credit use and behavior. Paying loans on time and staying well below your credit limit helps you get and keep good credit scores.

 Consumer Financial Protection Bureau

See more about managing credit at consumerfinance.gov

Hudkins Publishing

Phoenix, AZ

If you found this report to be helpful, please share the webpage from where it was obtained on social media. Thank you.